ALEXIS KARPOUZOS

AN OCEAN OF SOULS

MYSTIC POETRY

AF443829

Alexis karpouzos is an internationally recognized Philosopher,

Spiritual Teacher and Author. He is the Founder of the International

Community of Learning, Research and Culture in Greece.

Alexis karpouzos has published twelve books in Greek and four in English:

1.The self-criticism of science,

2. Cosmology: philosophy and physics,

3. Universal consciousness:

The bridges between science and spirituality,

4. The end of certainty.

Other Publications of Alexis karpouzos

- Introduction to philosophy of Understanding, The adventure of

human emancipation, Free Press

-The Philosophy of Nature, Free Press

Universal consciousness, Cosmic Spirit

Non- Duality, Cosmic Spirit

Cosmology, philosophy and Physics, Think Lab

-The languages of the world, the worlds of language, Think. Lab

Upcoming publications

-Time and Thought

- Technique and Time

TABLE OF CONTENTS

CHAPTER 1

BEYOND THE HEAVEN

Beyond the heaven

there is the country of heart,

here dwells the deepest secret nobody
knows,

here the bud sees the bud,

the mind can't hide its darkness

and the shadow of the soul is
illuminated,

and this is the miracle

that's keeping the stars in harmony
orbit.

1

A NEW ARRIVAL

Our life a dazzling dream and the death a new
arrival,

there is no end and never was a beginning.

Thousand centuries will gone

and will leave faint signs in the breaths of time,

thousand suns will light up

and will burst and unexpected visitors

will come and will gone

but something innate in us knows, we were, we
are,

and will be forever,

a timeless gentle touch in eternity's face.

2

IS OUR FATE

I know that I shall meet my shadow, one day, is our fate.

I know that, someday, the light ends for us

And the deadly gravity will absorb us.

And again, a magician spark will shine

and a ocean of souls will flood the universe

and will give birth to stars and grief.

And maybe, just maybe, in another heaven,

my dreams will be your dreams.

You see, everything repeats itself

and everything will be reincarnated in different forms.

An incredible miracle, carefree, and we live in it.

The miracle is folded into your heart.

3

THE GREAT WELCOME

This morning I walked the road of awe.

I met frustrated gods and angels sad.

The people had abandoned them

and the magic had tumbled.

Now, the people are orphans,

wanderers across the night,

frightened meteors looking for the source.

"Where to look for it?"

"Don't look away.

The sanctuary manifested in the bird

that wakes the sun in the morning with its song,

in the raindrop that narrates the sorrows of the
sky,

in the air that whispers secrets in the trees,

in the arrival of sparrows".

Sanctuary, the Great Welcome.

4

LOVE IS YOUR WINGS

I saw an angel on heaven

and he invited me to be neighbors to the stars.

"How can I fly? I don't have wings".

"I know you're encased in an old human's body

with frozen souls and unused magical dreams".

"But remember, you know quite well,

deep within you,

that there is only a single magic,

a single power and that is called loving.

Love is Your wings".

I MET A WORD

Last night,

in my dream, while I wandering in the wild lands

and crossing silent shadows,

i met a word and ask: ''What's your name?

''My name is love and I'm alone in life, I need you,

otherwise will be lost the dream''.

I answered: ''We need you too,

but we are in pain and scared and don't admit it.

Please, lend me your glowing eyes''.

''No, no need,

you're in the embrace of light,

but you've forgotten it''.

6

I ASK THE LIPS

I ask the lips,

why are you crying?

'I lost my color, i lost my flame, i lost my longing'.

The eye says: 'I lost the inward tenderness,

fade the light around me'

and the ear, 'i don't hear harmonies

but lamentations and screams.

And the heart whispers:

'Finally, the breeze will continue

to lightly caresses the night sky

and the clouds will dissolve.

Pain itself will crack the rock and let the soul

emerge'.

7

WHERE IS THE MAGIC?

Where is the magic?
We all start out knowing magic,

We are born with hurricanes and whirlwinds,

oceans and galaxies inside us.

We are able to sing to birds and read the clouds

and see the destiny in grains of sand.

But we have forgotten the magic

and we feel without compass, alone and
desperately,

only selfishness, only pain, fear and darkness.

But, magic of love has never disappeared from the
life,

the love holds the life.

8

WHEN THE BIRDS

When the birds take back their language,

when the trees unloose

their tenderly hands from around you,

when the air doesn't breathe

and the seas are tearing,

when the flowers whisper:

No, you own nothing,

then remember:

Your visitor, honoring the hospitality.

THANK YOU, SUN

Thank you, sun,

to be where you are in the universe,

to keep us from ever-darkness,

to ease us with warm touching,

to hold us in the great hands of light.

Thank you because never said on Earth "You own me".

HELLO SUN.

10

YOU'RE DRENCHED IN MAGIC

You came in to this world with enough light

to find your way out of the dark,

enough kindness to save a soul,

enough love to shift a planet.

Don't worry,

you are equipped with all you could ever need.

Look with in,

You are drenched in magic.

THE GREAT POETRY

Come from the depths of infinity

and from all directions of space-time.
I traveled through dark tunnels,

went through solar storms.
I went straight, circled, parallel, rotated as a spiral.
Cosmic clouds trapped me and escaped from
them.
Avoided collisions with meteorites.
I was helped by exotic particles,

neutron stars and the love of gravity.
Every leaf, every flower, every mountain and lake,
every cloud and every star and every atom

recognize me and greet me.
I feel that i have live for million lifetimes.

Who am i? What is my purpose?
Last night i sent a question into universe,

asking" who am I or am i not?
The universe responded immediately:
"You asked me the same thing billions of years
ago.
And then and now I answer:
You're the smile of no birth and no death.
The Great promise"!

12

WE NEED A SACRED TEAR

Dust to dust by the broken dreams of the

humanity,

you aren't got a lot to say, the words are sad,

now, our companion, the pains of the heart.

The indifference kills with no shame or concern,

killing me, killing you,

watch the end of the blessing,.

But, one day, the sun stopped,

the rain stopped falling,

the flowers didn't look high,

the sky emptied of stars

then a tear dripped from the heart

and became our breath.

We need a sacred tear,

before the fall.

13

I SAW A LITTLE LEAF

I saw a little leaf to whirling in the wind

didn't want to fall from the tree

but the leaf keeps falling over,

i prop it up, it falls again.

At the end,

the heartbroken leaf leaves a tear when it falls

and say goodbye to the tree.

That little leaf reincarnated into the earth

and started vits cycle all over again.

Little leaf, the storyteller of our life.

FALLEN ANGEL

Fallen angel!

Why are you scared?

Why you dwelt alone in shadow?

Why you tighten your fists?

why threaten the whole life?

i know, afraid to love,

let tenderness pour from your eyes to irrigate the
earth

and the light of love,

silently,

will lift you on the heaven again.

15

LOVE SAID ME

Love said me,

the love happens all the time in heaven.

Why not in the earth?

Human, take my hand,

you don't remember the dream of love,

but the great dream of our heart remembers us,

as the sun are there even and the earth turns,

until the end of the world.

16

THE MAST OF LIFE

You can hear the earth sigh,

the shadow is chasing us, the fear embodied us.

But the hunter of all shadows

dressed in the sun's morning ray

will continue to weave the mast of life

and like seeds that dreaming beneath the ground

your heart is still free to dreams.

17

GIVE YOUR SMILE

and like seeds that dreaming beneath the ground

your heart is still free to dreams.

17

GIVE YOUR SMILE

16

THE MAST OF LIFE

You can hear the earth sigh,

the shadow is chasing us, the fear embodied us.

But the hunter of all shadows

dressed in the sun's morning ray

will continue to weave the mast of life

through our heart journey's the eternity unfolds

and encircles us with her gentle hands,

there is no end or return,

no answer,

just one spark flickers.

20

DON'T SAY

19

THE EARTH IS OUR HEAVEN

We are the beat of nature's heart,

the earth is our heaven

and the sun our breath,

THE TIME HAS COME

The time has come to give back our heart to itself,

to light the spark to eye,

to stay vigil with yearning on lips,

so, open your wings,

beat your feathers

and will rising again on the heaven,

on the heaven which only is higher than the heaven.

Our souls are tied across universes,

there is unbroken continuity,

you see the love is more powerful than death,

so, let the winds of the heavens to dance with you

and give your smile at the other's welcome

Don't say

I'm iinsignificant in the infinite,

don't say

I'm alone in life,

you are a cosmic collection

that dances harmoniously.

You coexist with all beings,

visible and invisible together,

you are bound from the energy

of the universe itself.

WE ARE MADE OF HEAVEN

We are made of heaven,

risen from the tears of fallen stars

and from the songs of silence.

We met on the flying rock

and remembered that our hearts

we're beating at the same rhythm,

twin stars of different births.

22

OUR EXISTENCE HAS NO END

We live eternal amid the moment,

we live in the whispers through the heavens,

we live in particles of sunlight,

we live in every dimension of time

and in every direction of space,

our existence has no end.

23

DON'T TELL ME

Don't tell me the stars stopped to dream.

Don't tell me the birds don't fly.

Don't tell me the kid stopped crying.

Don't tell me the lovers are lost.

Observes the wonders as they occur around you.

Listen blessings dropping their blossoms around
you.

THE BREATH OF LIGHT

We are the gleam of infinite,

the breath of light,

the spark of life,

the chain of being,

the circle of the spheres the scale of creation,

the rise and the fall.

We are what we are and we are not.

We are the soul in all.

I DREAM

I dream that one day

we will look at each other

in the same way we look at the sun,

and we will touch each other

like the sun on earth,

and the blessings of light

will flow into our hearts.

26

THE SOUL OF ETERNITY

We are the body of heaven

and the soul of eternity,

the desolation and pains of hell are within us,

the joy and pleasures of paradise also.

We finish at the start

and with ending we begins

in the infinity of space-time, the celestial ash
wander.

WE ARE A SORT POEM

We are a short poem

in an endless emptiness page,

words are lighthouses that ignites

and struggle to deliver light

to the dark edges of the infinite,

and mystic sounds struggle

to give voice to the unlived beings,

to bore a young soul to the gate of birth.

28

EVERY LIFE

Every life dwell in the bosom of the
love,

echoing the bliss of eternity,

ringing as a heavenly gong the holy song,

the song of love wherewith even hell had thrilled

and the grief ignites,

and the eager souls lean to hear with awe.

29

BEYOND THE VISIBLE

And if the people ceased to hear you,

and when the words are fall silent,

who says that all vanish?

Beyond the visible,

there is a dream that i come from,

no shade, a dream who never changes my love.

This dream where we really live

is the face of everyone i see.

I LOVED THE LOVE

I loved the love and i still love of it,

because it's a light break in endless darkness,

the lake that awaits you on the desert,

the rose that cannot wither,

the warm nest of birds

Love, between hello and goodbye we never are alone.

31

KISS THE STARS

When in the world grows the dark cold

and the empty desolation,

then going back where one starts from.

Do you recall the longing of our wishes?

It is time, rise up to meet the heaven,

to kiss the stars,

to wrap your arms around the light.

32

FIND THE DREAM

'I'm afraid that when gone away from this life,

I will haven't yet to find anything beautiful and truth.

"We are astray, we are deluded, we have no hope".

"look deeper, way below the anger, the hate,

the jealousy way down deeper where the dream life.

Find the Dream".

UNDENIABLE MIRACLE

A sun kissed morning,

the love lightens the limitless sky as it rises and the
rays as ribbons of light

and color fall slowly from the sky,

silently a flower bloom,

the birds excited,

mountains touch seas that bathes the soil.

Undeniable miracle.

34

.

LOVE WAS BORN

The stars blink in awe

when the soul gleam from love,

of the gleam of souls,

the celestial light bursts forth

and life miracles radiate in eternity.

Love was born and set the worlds alight.

35

THE HIDDEN LAW

The soul goes out alone on oceans unknown,

stripped of all golden myths,

now,

the golden selfishness and arrogance will fade

and truth will shine through death,

we are a little dust,

who loves,

is our nature.

The hidden law comes back.

THE HEAVEN DARKENED

The heaven darkened,

heavy clouds on the way,

earth is crying,

but before, now and after,

through the emptiness,

there are unspeakable worlds,

unwritten poems and passionate intensity,

Love comes on unexpectedly

in the middle of the night.

I LOVE A FLOWER

I love a flower,

I stretch my hand

and touch his soft leaves

and it sends me a sweet smell.

it's a tacit love,

in the sense of wonder we found in each other,

secret signals from another life

that bring poetry to my heart.

LITTLE BY LITTLE

Little by little,

we will turn into stars,

little by little,

we will turn into the infinite universe,

little by little,

we will spin in eternal ecstasy,

hand in hand, pure love that flows.

39

WE ARE DREAMS GUESTS

The fate whispered our names,

our future,

molding our life,

leaving fingerprints all over a humanity soul,

and reminded us our limitations

that nothing could separate us from nature's life,

we aren't owners and conquerors of life,

we are dreams guests.

SO MANY ROADS

In our brief life,

so many roads,

so many miracles and blessings and glories,

but also, so many curses and denials,

grief and contempt,

continuous waves on the planetary seas that come
and go,

and they crawl us into the vast heavens,

in that quiet rhythm universe

listen to your heart beat.

41

CHAPTER 4
LOVE POEMS

BE THERE

I will find you in the shadow of words,

in the hidden signs

of silent moments,

in the eloquence of your eyes,

in a tingling in the spine,

in a trembling in the voice,

in a distant memory,

be there....

COME TO ME

Come to me wearing all your scars,

come to me bring the divine tears of despair

and the darkness of your fall,

you see I want it all from you,

don't worry,

the softness of our lips will change the fate.

43

THE TUNE OF ETERNITY

I will light up the heavens

just with your kisses

and thousand suns will flow on thee,

the divine shiver will wrap your body,

the fire of eternity will burn every drop of your blood.

Now, your heart will be stopped

and will start to beat on the tune of eternity.

I WANT YOUR TOUCH

I want your touch.

I want your voice and your thoughts.

I want your grace and your mistakes.

I want your passion and your fears.

I want everything.

I want everything in her.

The stardust that makes her

is the same stardust that makes me.

45

FROM LOVE

From love,

fire becomes light,

from love, sorrow becomes joy,

from love, fury becomes mercy,

from love, thorns become flowers,

from love, sickness becomes health,

from love, dead becomes alive.

Love, just how the sun shines on to our world,

without any exception.

46

THE HEAT OF UNITY

Show me where the fairies hide
messages,

show me treasures and feathers,

show me how to run again barefoot with empty
pockets.

Lead me under the sun

and let me to glide in brightness.

Let me to feel the amorous heat of unity.

47

THE LIFE'S WALTZ

You are us and we are you and yet together,

dreams that dream in eternity's hug,

suddenly,

atoms are connected and acquire language,

the breath will craft the context,

the words uttered will makes a world to appear,

and the tune of punctuation is the life's waltz.

THE ABYSS OF INFINITY

Stars scattered everywhere,

tell stories from ancient times

their breathing connects the earth and heaven

and dreams are born,

to the forbidden abyss of infinity,

silently a flower bloom.

49

THE BLISS OF ETERNITY

At least, above us, stars shine,

tiny pieces of heaven

that overflowing with happiness

and absorb our tiredness.

Every heart's a star within,

that echoing the bliss of eternity.

every star's an aflame heart

that holds our hand.

FACE TO FACE

Face to face,

earth and heaven,

eternal lovers,

talking each other through the light,

infinite distances between them,

but a wonderful living side by side.

This silent poem speaks to us,

before we are and it will continue after us.

51

WORLDS OF MIRACLES

Darkness at the shut of day,

broken hearts

and silent tears around me the words are sad,

the clocks stopped,

but the light from a dead star will live in infinity,

its rays will continue to cross the vast starry
heavens

and they will illuminate worlds of miracles.

52

IN THE MIDDLE OF THE NIGHT

The heaven darkened,

heavy clouds on the way,

earth is crying,

but before, now and after,

through the emptiness,

there are unspeakable worlds,

unwritten poems and passionate intensity,

Love comes on unexpectedly in the middle of the
night.

TIME HAS COME

The time has come to give back our heart to itself,

to light the spark to eye,

to stay vigil with yearning on lips so,

open your wings,

beat your feathers

and will rising again on the heaven,

on the heaven which only is higher than the
heaven,

www.ingramcontent.com/pod-product-compliance
Lightning Source LLC
Chambersburg PA
CBHW031213160726
47992CB00006B/2715